A NOTE TO PARENTS ABOUT BREAKING PROMISES

"But, you promised!" Few children make it through childhood without directing this lament to someone who has broken a promise. Broken promises, no matter how large or small, are destructive. They erode the trust necessary to build and maintain secure human relationships.

The purpose of this book is to teach children the importance of being someone who can be trusted. In addition, it teaches children how to be trustworthy by keeping whatever promises they make.

Because it is almost impossible to have a positive relationship with someone who can not be trusted, children need to learn that trustworthiness is one of the most valuable assets that they can bring to a relationship.

When you break a promise, you teach your child that promises are meaningless. When you keep a promise, you teach your child that promises are important. Therefore, when it comes to promises, it is essential that you model the attitudes and behavior you wish to teach your child. In order to make sure you keep your promises, it is crucial that you make only the ones you are certain you can keep.

A Children's Book About

BREAKING PROMISES

Managing Editor: Ellen Klarberg
Copy Editor: Annette Gooch
Editorial Assistant: Lana Eberhard
Art Director: Jennifer Wiezel
Production Artist: Gail Miller
Illustration Designer: Bartholomew
Inking Artist: Barbara Baird
Coloring Artist: Berenice Happé Iriks
Lettering Artist: Linda Hanney
Typographer: Communication Graphics

A Children's Book About

BREAKING PROMISES

By Joy Berry

GROLIER
B O O K S

GROLIER BOOKS IS A DIVISION OF GROLIER ENTERPRISES, INC.

This book is about Sam.

Reading about Sam can help you understand and deal with **breaking promises.**

Have your friends ever failed to do
something they promised they would do?

?

Have your parents or other adults ever
failed to do something they promised they
would do?

People break a promise when they fail to do something they promised to do.

When someone breaks a promise:
- How do you feel?
- What do you think?
- What do you do?

When someone breaks a promise:
- You might feel disappointed, frustrated, and angry.
- You might think the person cannot be trusted.
- You might not believe the person any more.

It is important not to break the promises you make. People can trust you if you keep your promises.

People can depend on you when they can trust you. They know you will not let them down. They know you will be honest and not lie.

People will believe what you say if they can trust you. They will allow you to do more on your own.

You must show people you can be trusted
if you want them to trust you.

Show people you can be trusted. *Be where you say you will be.*

Show people you can be trusted. *Do what you say you will do.*

Show people you can be trusted. *Give what you say you will give.*

You must keep your promises if you want to be trusted.

It is important to treat people the way you want to be treated.

You should keep your promises if you want other people to keep theirs.